# MAKING
# YouTube
# VIDEOS

Nick Willougby

**WILEY**

## MAKING YOUTUBE® VIDEOS

Published by
John Wiley & Sons, Inc.
111 River Street
Hoboken, NJ 07030-5774

www.wiley.com

For general information on our other products and services, please contact our Customer Care Department within the U.S. at 877-762-2974, outside the U.S. at 317-572-3993, or fax 317-572-4002. For technical support, please visit www.wiley.com/techsupport.

Wiley publishes in a variety of print and electronic formats and by print-on-demand. Some material included with standard print versions of this book may not be included in e-books or in print-on-demand. If this book refers to media such as a CD or DVD that is not included in the version you purchased, you may download this material at http://booksupport.wiley.com. For more information about Wiley products, visit www.wiley.com.

Library of Congress Control Number: 2015947350

ISBN 978-1-119-17724-1 (pbk); ISBN 978-1-119-17725-8 (ebk); ISBN 978-1-119-17726-5 (ebk)

This book was produced using the Myriad Pro typeface for the body text and callouts, and Bangers for the chapter titles and subheads.

Manufactured in the United States of America

10 9 8 7 6 5 4 3 2

# CONTENTS

## PROJECT 3: EDIT                           68

# INTRODUCTION

### HELLO FUTURE YOUTUBERS!

Welcome to *Making YouTube Videos* — the book that does exactly what it says on the cover.

You want to be the next YouTube star? Do you find yourself watching YouTube videos and thinking, "I could do that!" Or, "I really want to do that!" Well, you've picked up the right book.

Millions of people are uploading their videos to YouTube — and there's plenty of room for you, too. All you need is to turn the creative ideas in your head into videos. You're going to have so much fun and I'm going to guide you through every step.

## ABOUT YOUTUBE

YouTube started in 2005 for people all over the world to share videos. I don't think anyone guessed how successful it would become. Would you have guessed it?

Now if you want to learn how to do something or watch funny videos, where do you go? YouTube. And did you know that some people make YouTube videos as a job? How fun would that be?

*Your safety is the most important thing. Don't include any personal information in the videos that you share on YouTube. Don't tell anyone online what your name is or where you live.*

## ABOUT THIS BOOK

They don't teach you how to make YouTube videos at school, do they? If they do, you go to an awesome school. In *Making YouTube Videos* I share what I've learned to help you make films. (I wish I'd had this book when I was a kid. That would be impossible, of course, unless I had a time machine for me and for YouTube.)

They say a wise person learns from his mistakes and a clever person learns from other people's mistakes. I've learned everything I know from working in different parts within the filmmaking industry, and the mistakes I made along the way made me better. The great thing is that you get to avoid making a bunch of the mistakes that I made.

In this book, you

- » Explore the different cameras you can use.
- » Discover how to record sound.
- » Find out how to light your scenes.
- » Edit your video.
- » See ways to share your videos on YouTube.

Sometimes you'll see a URL (web address) for forms or examples I put online for you. You can find those extras at www.dummies. com/go/makingyoutubevideos.

Some figures will have a magnifying glass, like you see here. The glass is drawing attention to the parts of the screen that you use. The highlighted text draws your attention to the figure.

## ABOUT YOU

You're interested in making movies. That's why you're here reading this, right?

I also figure that you have a way to capture film (a camera or phone) and a way to edit it (a computer or laptop).

I bet you've been online before and know all about clicking icons, and that you've pressed the Record button on a camera.

## *ABOUT THE ICONS*

As you read through the projects in this book, you'll see a few icons. The icons point out different things:

*If something could be dangerous, or if it's something you shouldn't choose, you see this Warning icon.*

*The Remember icon gives you the most important things. This is information you'll use all the time when making films.*

*I use the Tip icon when I have information or advice that could help you with your film project.*

### DID YOU KNOW THERE ARE BILLIONS OF VIDEOS ON YOUTUBE?

Billions! And that people add 300 hours of video every minute? That's a lot of videos.

YouTube is a great way to share with your friends and family the videos you make. Don't worry if you haven't made a video yet. I'm going to help you make your very own YouTube video as you read this book.

# FOLLOW THE VIDEO-MAKING PROCESS

You can divide the video-making process into five main stages:

» Development

» Pre-production

» Production

» Post-production

» Distribution

If you imagine the video-making process as a trip, these five main stages are stops on the way. You can't get where you're going unless you go to each place along the way.

## DEVELOPMENT

*Development* is one of the most important areas of the process — and it can be one of the hardest, too. It's usually the longest part of video making, because it's important to get the concept and the story right before moving into pre-production.

The development stage means

» Creating ideas and coming up with themes to create a story that has a good beginning, middle, and end.

» Building the story so that it's ready to take into pre-production. Writing a script for the actors to work from and, sometimes, a storyboard for the director and crew to work from. A *storyboard* is a series of images that help you plan which shots you're going to film.

## PRE-PRODUCTION

This stage uses the idea, story, script, and storyboard to prepare for the production stage. In pre-production, everything is planned as much as possible.

*If you rush or skip pre-production, something may go wrong and it could take you longer to film.*

*Pre-production* is when you

» Choose actors.

» Find locations.

» Build sets for each scene.

» Plan each filming day.

» Organize rehearsals for the actors.

The work you do on these steps saves you time in the production and post-production stages.

## PRODUCTION

The production stage is where the story and characters come to life as you film.

The *production* stage is when you

» Run rehearsals for the actors to learn their lines and to develop their characters.

» Set up camera equipment on location.

» Film the scenes you planned.

» Review the filmed footage to make sure you've captured everything and that it looks good enough to edit.

## POST-PRODUCTION

The *post-production* stage is when you piece together the footage you captured during production. This stage is exciting.

You get to see your hard work put into the previous stages and to watch the video come together in the editing tool.

*Post-production* includes

» Importing the footage on a computer.

» Editing in software like iMovie or Movie Maker.

» Adding music, sound effects, and other kinds of effects.

## DISTRIBUTION

*Distribution* is the final stage in the journey. At this point, your film has been produced and edited. Now it's ready for the audience to enjoy.

This can be a worrisome time for you because the audience will make comments and give reviews.

Most blockbuster films are first distributed to theaters and then released on DVD, but you'll distribute your video by YouTube.

## GET YOUR TOOLS

A professional filmmaker could spend a fortune on tools. However, to get started you only need a few basic tools, and most of them are not that expensive:

» **Video camera:** Without a video camera, there is no video. A video camera captures the picture and audio and stores them on a media card, hard drive, or tape. You can read more about cameras in the next section.

» **Microphone:** The microphone records sound on a media card, hard drive, or tape. The microphone could be built into your camera or not (and in that case it's *external*). Project 2 teaches you more about using a microphone for audio.

» **Light source:** Your audience needs to see your subjects, so light is quite important. The source could be a natural one

# HOW YOUR CAMERA WORKS

Don't worry. I'm not going to bore you with details here — but it is useful to know the basics.

A video camera works a lot like your eye. Your eyes see things as a series of still images or *frames*. Your brain then puts them together so fast that it looks like smooth movement — it's clever stuff, isn't it? The camera does a very similar thing: It captures movement in a series of frames or still images.

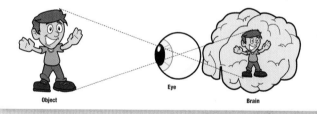

Object                    Eye                    Brain

Also like your eye, the camera records the images using light from the scene. The light enters through the lens and the images go on a microchip inside the digital video camera. These images go to your media card or tape.

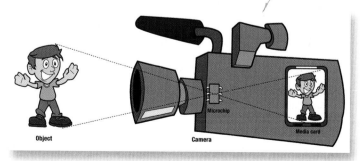

Object          Microchip    Camera          Media card

(like the sun) or an artificial one (like a lamp). Project 2 helps you with lighting.

» **Editing tool:** An editing tool is a computer program where you import video footage, slice it up, and arrange it. Project 3 is all about editing.

» **Tripod:** A tripod is a great tool for keeping the camera steady in a *fixed* (single) position. It can be used to smoothly film moving subjects from left to right or up and down.

» **Media card/tape:** This is where your camera stores video footage.

» **Headphones:** You can plug this device into a video camera or external sound recorder to monitor the *quality* of the audio. How good is it?

## CHOOSE YOUR CAMERA

Digital video cameras make filmmaking easier and less expensive. They come in different sizes, qualities, and prices. For under $100, you can buy a compact HD

## CHECK YOUR TEMPERATURE

This may sound odd, but light comes in different colors. A candle has a warm orange look. A clear blue sky has a colder blue look. The color of light is measured in a unit called *Kelvin*. You can adjust this setting on your camera using the white balance, or by simply setting your camera to auto white balance. This adjusts the color temperature for you to match the light in your scene.

## BACK IN THE OLD DAYS

Traditional film cameras captured footage as a bunch of still images. The images were on light-sensitive tape running through the camera. This reel of tape was expensive to buy and you couldn't reuse it. It also made it tough to set up and check shots.

Traditional film cameras create what I call a *cinematic* look, which makes the image look softer than you can with digital video. With traditional cameras you can, for example, blur backgrounds and make your subject stand out. It's harder to get this cinematic look with a digital video camera, especially with less expensive camcorders, which often have trouble with the lighter and darker areas of a shot, and whose images tend to be sharper.

camcorder that records great video. Because you're starting out, this is completely reasonable.

*HD (high-definition)* cameras have better quality images than the old *standard definition (SD)*. HD has better detail and brighter colors.

At the other extreme, you can find video cameras that cost over $50,000. Professionals use those cameras to shoot blockbuster movies — but even those cameras have downsides.

As a filmmaker, I like to use different types of digital video cameras for different reasons. The following sections describe the different types of digital video cameras.

## WEBCAMS

A *webcam* plugs directly into your computer. They're affordable, easy to set up, and great for recording someone talking to the computer. Most desktop computers and laptops come with webcams.

If you want to film your YouTube video using a webcam but your computer doesn't have one built in, look online or in stores. They start around $20.

I use a webcam to record video blogs because webcams are simple to set up. They make it easy to edit and upload in a shorter amount of time.

## CAMERA PHONES

A *camera phone* is a cell phone that captures still and moving images. Camera phones are smaller and lighter, which makes it easier to capture video in smaller spaces.

Camera phones don't offer the best quality for picture or sound, but they're great for capturing video simply and quickly.

## SOMETIMES ONE IS BETTER THAN TWO

For years, cameras used two lenses — one through which the photo was captured on film, and another that passed the image to the *viewfinder* (which is what the photographer looks through). This approach had some problems. Sometimes photographers didn't get the pictures they thought they were getting. The single-lens reflex camera (and later, the digital single-lens reflex camera, or DSLR) changed that: With the single lens, the image you see through the viewfinder is the same as what you get in pictures.

*Because camera phones are perfect for capturing random moments that you can't with a larger camera, I use them to capture video and pictures for behind-the-scenes projects.*

## CAMCORDERS

A *camcorder* is a handheld video camera designed to record video and audio. Camcorders usually have lenses built in and make setting up and filming quicker and easier. Over the years, they've become less expensive and offer better video and sound quality than ever.

There are many types of camcorders to choose from, starting with basic (around $100) going all the way up to broadcast cameras (over $50,000). You can put camcorders in two groups: affordable and professional.

I think affordable is the way to go!

## AFFORDABLE CAMCORDERS

The affordable range of camcorders offers some great features and fantastic quality. Most of the cameras in this group offer "automatic" functions like this:

» Autofocus, which focuses on the subject instead of the background.

» Face detection, which focuses on the people in the shot.

» Auto-iris, which adjusts brightness, depending on the light.

» Auto white-balance, which adjusts the color temperature of the video image.

Camcorders in this range are small, light, and easy to work with. They're great for shooting home videos.

## PROFESSIONAL CAMCORDERS

I suppose I could have called this section "Unaffordable camcorders." Professional filmmakers need more from their cameras than most mere mortals do. Professionals sometimes need to take manual control and bypass the camcorder's brain altogether. We all know people are smarter than computers.

Who uses these fancy things? Teams recording outside news and production companies for the movies you'll see at the local theater.

Usually, the higher you go up in the range of professional camcorders, the bigger the cameras get and the more manual features they have. The bigger camcorders are heavy! Twenty pounds may not sound like a lot, but it gets tough carrying that weight around and trying to hold it steady for long.

## ACTION CAMERAS

Camera makers are fitting more stuff into less space. This leads to *action cameras*, which are very small, light camcorders that you can strap to yourself, sports equipment, bikes, cars, and even your dog.

With an action camera, you can record video that's usually hard to get. For example, a cyclist can attach an action camera to her helmet to record what she sees as she's cycling. Action cameras can also be attached to free runners, skiers, sky divers, and race-car drivers. The footage from action cameras helps the audience feel involved.

Action cameras are a great, inexpensive way to capture high-quality video. You can pay as little as $50 for one.

*An action camera doesn't have the best sound. These cameras are for shots where you don't need or care much about audio.*

## AERIAL CAMERAS

Shots filmed from the sky can look amazing, and they're being used more often in film and TV. You can get aerial video by attaching cameras to drones or quadcopters, and get stunning footage that you can't see from the ground.

Before drones and quadcopters were around, the only way to get footage from the sky was by taking a camera up in a full-size helicopter. That isn't cheap. Aerial cameras give the same effect for a lot less money.

Lots of drones and quadcopters are for sale at camera stores, and most start around $50.

*In some places, you need a license to fly a drone or quadcopter. Make sure you know what the rules are where you live.*

## DSLR VIDEO

Basically, a *DSLR camera* is one that uses a mirror behind the lens to reflect what's happening through the lens into the eyepiece. The DSLR is a still-photography camera that uses detachable lenses and produces some amazing images. Within the past ten years or so, the makers began including a video function with their DSLR cameras that allows you to capture beautiful video, too.

*DSLR cameras are more compact than some digital cinema cameras, so they're great if you're traveling or shooting in small spaces.*

DSLR video can look very *cinematic*, which means it looks more like the quality you'd see in a blockbuster film at the theater.

» They have bigger sensors, which capture more of the scene — more light and a greater depth of field. *Depth of field* is the area of your shot that's in focus. A large depth of field has more of your shot in focus. A shallow depth of field has less of your shot in focus (so the area behind and in front of your subject may look blurry).

» They allow different lenses so you can get a variety of shots. The different shots are explained in more detail in the next project.

*DSLRs aren't great for recording long video clips. They can overheat, so they have a limited recording time.*

Recording sound isn't easy, either. The built-in microphone is so-so at best. The camera makes quite a bit of noise while you're recording; the only way to connect an external microphone is through a mini jack.

I used DSLR cameras for video when they were first released and I've shot many short films using them. The video was great, but because of the DSLR's limits with sound, I recorded sound using a separate device and then matched the sound to the video later, during the editing process. If you're working on a large project, matching sound like this can take a long time.

## DIGITAL CINEMA CAMERAS

*Digital cinema cameras* are used to film larger projects and they give a more cinematic look. Like camcorders, digital cinema cameras have become more affordable and smaller. Fifty years ago, you would've needed a truck to carry around your cinema camera and equipment, but now it can fit into your backpack.

You can buy a digital cinema camera from most large camera stores, and they range in price from $1,000 to more than $60,000. Yeah. That isn't a misprint. That's more than a lot of cars cost.

Even though they can fit into your backpack, digital cinema cameras are usually bigger than most cameras. They are also usually the more expensive option: You buy the body of the camera and then buy attachments, including lenses and monitors. Some of these attachments cost as much as the camera body.

Cinema cameras tend to have more manual settings and can be complicated to set up. Because of this, I mainly use my cinema camera for dramas and projects that I do for businesses.

# PROJECT **2** *SHOOT*

### *BEFORE YOU PRESS THE RECORD BUTTON, GET PREPARED.*
Good preparation makes the other steps much easier. You prepare by choosing a style, creating an idea, and planning the shots.

Are you ready?

# CHOOSE A STYLE

An idea. A theme.

What do you want to make a video about? What do you want it to do? Coming up with an idea can be one of the hardest parts of making videos, but it can be the most exciting, too.

Now's the time to decide on the type, or style. You could make these popular types:

» **How-to's or tutorials.** If you have a skill that you'd like to show, you could create a how-to, or *tutorial,* video. It might be showing people how to play a song on the guitar or make an origami swan or put on make-up. Not much is off limits here.

» **Gaming or let's play.** If you're a gamer and want to show other people how good (or bad) you are at playing, you could create a let's play video. Maybe you have some tips you want to share?

 *Filming a gaming or let's-play video means you need to be able to record and capture the game footage and send it into an editing tool. If you're a Mac user, you can use the screen recording function in QuickTime player. If you're a PC user, you can download a free screen-capture tool from www.ezvid.com.*

» **Review.** Here's a great way to tell your YouTube audience what you think or how you feel. You could review a camera you bought or a film you watched or a place you visited. Even a recipe you tried! You could include photos and video clips of the product you're reviewing.

» **Funny.** You have probably seen loads of funny animal videos on YouTube, especially starring cats. Cats in boxes, cats taking selfies, cats taking naps, and many, many more cats.

## ASK PERMISSION FIRST

Getting permission to film people is really
important. You don't want someone
you've filmed to change his mind and
demand to be taken out — especially after you've
finished editing and uploading the film to YouTube.
To avoid this problem, ask the people in your film
to complete a *model release form*. By signing the
form, they agree that you can use their image in your
film. After they sign the release, they give up the
right to change their minds later. I use a standard
model release form. You can get a blank version at
www.dummies.com/go/makingyoutubevideos.

People often record these videos with camera phones and
usually, they're events that can't be repeated. Does your pet
do something funny?

» **Short films.** If you want to create a video that has a story
to it, and you want to work with actors and create scripts,
then making a short film is for you. Your film can be *fictional*
(made up) or *nonfictional* (true). For short films, you might
want to use a camcorder.

» **Video blogs.** If you want to talk to your audience about an
interesting topic or if you have an opinion about something,
you could create a video blog (also known as a *vlog*). Vlogs
are like video diaries and are usually filmed with webcams or
smaller video recording devices.

How you can make your video stand out? How will your video be
different?

## THINK OF AN IDEA

Coming up with an idea can be one of the hardest parts of making a video — but it can be the most exciting, too. I've spent days, weeks, and even months thinking of ideas for films. I've been driving my car or washing the dishes when an idea popped into my head.

When you've decided on a style, decide what your video is *about*.

Think about these questions when you're coming up with an idea:

» **What does your audience want?** Who *is* your audience? What do they want? Don't think just about what you want to do or what *you* think will work. Ask your audience — people you know who watch your sort of video. What would they like to see? Someone may give you the seed of an idea that you could help grow into something amazing.

» **What stories are out there?** Many films and videos are based on true stories. Do you or someone you know have a story worth telling? Ask around. See what you can find. Most of the films I've written are based on things that have happened to me or people I know. If you can't find a story from people you know, look through a few short story books; they may inspire you.

» **What's possible?** Telling stories about aliens, monsters, and faraway planets can be good if you own a spaceship — but what kinds of stories can you film with the locations and props you already have? For inspiration, have a look around and see what's available to you.

Also, think about who can help make your video: Who will act? Who will hold the boom? It's okay to ask someone to help you write or brainstorm ideas. I've written a lot of films with a writing partner, which is great: One of us may come up with an idea, and the other person will throw in more ideas, and the story builds from there.

» **Is there a bad idea?** No. There's no such thing. Write down every idea you have. Any idea could become something great. You may write down loads of ideas you won't use for a while, but it never hurts to have more than you need. Any idea that's useless for your current project could well inspire your next story.

## STRUCTURE YOUR VIDEO

When planning your YouTube video, it might be helpful to create a *structure*.

*Every good story in every good video should have a good beginning, middle, and end. This applies to all video styles, including vlogs and tutorials.*

Think about the following stuff when you're structuring your video.

» **The introduction:** This is an important part of your video. It's when your audience decides to continue watching (or whether to bail out and do something else instead). Your introduction should *captivate* your audience — grab their attention — and make them want to watch. It should introduce your topic or theme and your characters.

» **The ending:** This is where you leave your audience, which is also really important. By the end of the video, your audience will form opinions. You want people who watch to turn to the next person and say, "That was good!" or "That was funny." To get that reaction, make sure you've given what you promised in the title or introduction. Did your audience learn anything? Did they laugh? Were they entertained? Your ending can include a thank you to the audience for watching. You also can ask them to watch your other videos, to comment, or to subscribe to your YouTube channel.

» **Characters:** Every video has characters, whether they're real or made up.  If your video uses actors to play characters, think about creating a profile for each character.

 A character profile *describes the characters in your video. Is he quiet, funny, naughty? Is she smart, grumpy, playful? A character profile helps your actors know how to play their characters.*

» **Emotions:** Audiences like to feel emotions. If you can make your audience laugh, cry, jump, you've won a great battle. Think of your favorite film. What makes it your favorite? Is it because it makes you feel happy or sad? That's what you want your audience to think about your video.

Watch some other YouTube videos. What works well? What made you laugh or cry? How was the video introduced and ended?

## SCRIPT YOUR VIDEO

I love writing scripts because that's the moment a video starts coming to life. Depending on what style you choose, you may want to write a script to explain each scene and create *dialogue* (lines for actors).

You can see how I wrote and arranged my script.

```
MILO TOOK MY PHONE

SCENE 1 - NICK'S INTRODUCTION
```

Action/direction ———
```
Nick is sitting at his desk talking to his webcam. He is
holding his phone in his hand.
```

Character name ——————————————————
```
                               NICK
```

Dialogue ——————
```
Hi. This is unbelievable! My phone
went missing yesterday and I've
just found it. When I looked
through my phone I couldn't believe
what I saw. It appears that Milo,
my dog, has taken my phone and
filmed himself. Don't believe me?
Well, here's what I found!
```

```
SCENE 2 - MILO ON SOFA

Milo is lying in his bed and is looking at phone. The phone
moves around to make it look like Milo is adjusting the
phone to frame himself. Milo's voiceover starts.

                         MILO VOICEOVER

Right, how do you work this
thing... There... Good... Hello.
I'm Milo and this is my bed. I lie
here most of the day as sleeping is
good. Anyway, I took my owner's
phone and thought I would make a
little film about my life. I do
hope you enjoy it.
```

If you're planning to create a short film using a story and lines for your actors, you may want to write a script. The script should have the following parts:

» **Action/direction.** This means descriptions of anything happening onscreen besides character dialogue. You can include shot information and notes for filming here, too. Action and direction could explain how an actor behaves or performs his character in a scene. An example of action and direction appears under the first scene heading, where it says "Nick is sitting at his desk talking to his webcam."

» **Character names.** Stick a character's name before her lines of dialogue so your actors know who's speaking.

» **Dialogue.** These are the words that you speak or that your characters speak. Make them as natural as possible. For example, in real life you'd say, "I'm sorry. I can't come tonight." Unless you're a super-formal person, you wouldn't say, "I am sorry that I cannot come tonight."

Using script software makes writing scripts a lot easier and quicker. It has *templates* (sort of like spaces already made) for arranging the action, character names, and dialogue. That makes it easier to read.

*I use software called Celtx, which you can download for free from www.celtx.com. Lots of other script-writing tools are available, or you can just use something like Word.*

*Scripting* can cut down the number of "ums" and "ers." You don't have to write a complete script for your vlog or tutorial, but it does help to make a list of points you want to talk about.

*It's important to plan what you're going to say, even if you're making a vlog or tutorial.*

# WRITE DIALOGUE

*Dialogue* is simply a conversation between your characters.

*The key to good dialogue is making it sound natural. Imagine what you'd say if you were the character. And you don't have to use dialogue to explain everything. Use facial expressions, body language, or actions to tell your story.*

*Read your dialogue out loud. If you stumble over a word, or if a line is hard to read, look for an easier way to say it.*

Dialogue can always change; your actors can say the same thing in their own way. This is okay, as long as the meaning doesn't change.

If you're having trouble thinking of what to write, try acting out your scene or reading out loud what you've already written. You also can ask a friend to help you write the dialogue for your YouTube video.

## MAKE A SHOT LIST

Creating a shot list will be one of the best things you can do to prepare for filming. Before you film a single thing, list the shots that you want to capture. A *shot list* helps you

» Keep track of what you've filmed.

» Plan the location, props, and actors for each shot.

*You may use the same location more than once but at different points in your film. For example, maybe you're at a park at the beginning and then at the ending of your film. Instead of filming those scenes on different days, film them on the same day.*

You can download a blank version of this shot list for your own video from www.dummies.com/go/makingyoutubevideos.

## Shot List

**Production Title:** 'Milo Took My Phone'

| Shot No. | Scene No. | Shot Type | Camera Movement | Description |
|---|---|---|---|---|
| 1 | 1 | Mid Shot | Fixed | Webcam shot of Nick at desk |
| 2 | 6 | Mid Shot | Fixed | Webcam shot of Nick at desk |
| 3 | 2 | Close Up | Handheld | Movement to look like Milo is holding camera |
| 4 | 3 | Close Up | Handheld | Movement. Include tilt up to see Nick (not looking at camera) |
| 5 | 4 | Mid Shot | Handheld | Milo's point of view of food |
| 6 | 4 | Close Up | Handheld | Movement to look like Milo is holding camera |
| 7 | 5 | Close Up | Handheld | Movement to look like Milo is holding camera |

A shot list has the following information:

» **Shot number** is the number of the shot in the order to be filmed. For example, the first shot that you want to film is shot 1, the second is shot 2, and the third is . . . you get it.

» **Scene number** shows the scene that the shot belongs to. You normally use this when referring to a script from a film with more than one scene. You might not need scene numbers if you're filming a vlog or how-to video. Scene 1 in my video was filmed using my webcam in my study, and I filmed scene 2, Milo in his bed, with my iPhone.

*A film is divided into scenes, which are a series of shots filmed in one location. As soon as the location changes, the scene changes.*

» **Shot type** is how close you'd like to capture your actors. For example, do you want a wide shot, mid shot, or close-up shot? I explain these in the next section.

» **Camera movement** is where you choose a fixed-camera position or camera movement. This is explained in more detail later in this project.

» **Shot description** is where you explain how the shot should look, with any notes to remember when filming. You may want to write notes on the type of camera movement or something you want your actors to do.

## CHOOSE A SHOT TYPE

*Choosing a shot type* refers to how your subject appears in the camera screen or viewfinder. By *framing a shot*, you choose what you see through the viewfinder on your camera and what your audience will see when it watches your film.

*Take time choosing your shots before you film anything. It saves time on the day of filming because you can get on with shooting rather than deciding what shots to use.*

» Some filmmakers choose shots before filming.

» Some filmmakers choose shots when they're creating a shot list, which comes after writing the script.

» Some filmmakers choose shots on the day they film, even though there are advantages to choosing shots ahead of time.

*I recommend choosing your shots before filming. It's less stressful and the results are usually better.*

You have lots of shots to choose from. In the following sections, I explain the different types and when to use them.

## WIDE SHOT

A *wide shot,* also known as a *long shot,* shows your audience more of the scene you're filming. Do this by zooming out on your camera or by moving your camera farther away from the subject or character.

Some filmmakers like to start scenes with a wide shot. This *establishing shot* shows more of the location or characters.

You can see that this shot is framed so that the horizontal line follows the line where the grass meets the trees.

Imagine that you want your audience to know that your characters are on a beach. You can begin with a wide shot showing your characters, the sky, the sea, and the sand. Hopefully, no sharks. Instantly your audience knows where the characters are.

*When you're framing a shot, look out for any straight lines you can find, either* horizontally *(side to side) or* vertically *(up and down) across the shot. Use these lines to keep your framing straight.*

**When should you use a wide shot?** Use it in a short film to show your audience the whole scene or when you're filming a funny video starring your pet.

## MID SHOT

The *mid shot,* or *medium shot,* frames the characters from a space above their heads to about halfway (*mid*way) down their bodies.

This shot is the most common on TV, film, and YouTube because it shows hand movements, gestures, and facial expressions. You want to capture that stuff.

The mid shot is used a lot in vlogs, reviews, and how to's because it focuses the audience's attention on the upper half of the body.

» A *two shot* is a mid shot used to film two people together. A two shot is often used in TV when two presenters host a show. You can try it in your YouTube videos if you have two characters side by side or face to face.

» *Over-the-shoulder shots* are great for conversations between characters who are facing each other. With an over-the-shoulder shot you see both characters at the same time, but only one character faces the camera.

I like to use over-the-shoulder shots because they let you see the expressions on a character's face. Because the character faces the viewer, these shots can make the audience feel like it's part of the conversation.

You may use an over-the-shoulder shot in your YouTube video if you are interviewing someone or if someone in your short film is having a conversation.

*With over-the-shoulder shots, it's common for actors to look at the camera. That can distract your audience. Move the camera farther away from the actor and then zoom in with the lens.*

**When should you use a mid shot?** When you're filming yourself talking about an interesting topic, or doing a review or vlog. I use my webcam to capture a mid shot of myself introducing my YouTube video about Milo.

## CLOSE-UP

Bringing the camera closer or zooming into your subject or character creates a *close-up shot*.

» A *cut-in* is a close-up shot used to show detail on an object or on a part of the subject that you can already see in the main scene — like a close-up of an actor's hands or of something an actor is holding.

The scene at the top of the next page shows a cut-in shot of one character passing over a key to another. In this scene, it is important that the audience see the key being passed from one character to another.

» An *extreme close-up* comes in even closer to your character (right in her mug!) or subject to show even more strong emotion or detail. If you want your audience to know that your character is really angry — hopping mad — you could use an extreme close-up of the actor's face to show the anger in her eyes.

**When should you use a close-up shot?** How about using a cut-in shot when you're filming a how-to video? Or when you want to show a character's facial expressions to help show emotions. You can use a close-up for any shot that requires more detail. For example, if you want to show the object in your character's hand, use a cut-in to a close-up shot of that object.

## CHOOSE MOVEMENT OR FIXED

Besides choosing how to frame your subject, think about whether you're going to mount your camera in a fixed position or move it around.

It's amazing how a small amount of movement from the camera can make a shot look more interesting and help build emotions.

» **Fixed-camera position** is when your camera is locked in one spot, without any movement. Normally for this you use a tripod. (See the "Steady does it! Using a tripod" sidebar to read more about that.) If you're creating a tutorial, how-to, or vlog, you may want to use a fixed-camera position with a webcam.

» **Moving camera** means you move your camera during the shot. This could be handheld or on a tripod. If you're filming your pet doing something funny, you might follow it using a camcorder.

# STEADY DOES IT! USING A TRIPOD

A tripod is a great tool for

» Keeping your shots steady

» Taking the weight of the camera off your camera operator

» Adding gentle movement to your shots

I like to film some shots on a tripod and some handheld because it can change the feeling through the video. What you choose depends on what feeling you want. Use a tripod if you want to give the scene a calm or relaxed feel, or if you want the audience to focus on the actors.

You *can* add movement to your shots with a tripod:

*Pan shots* move your camera horizontally on a tripod from right to left (or left to right). Don't pan too much within one shot. It can confuse the audience or make them uncomfortable. Don't use more than one pan per shot, if you need to at all.

*Tilt shots* move your camera vertically (up or down). You may want to use a tilt shot at the beginning of a scene to *establish,* or set up, the location. Too many tilt shots can be uncomfortable too. No more than one per scene.

You can see examples of tilt and pan shots at www.dummies.com/go/makingyoutubevideos.

*Filming a whole video with a handheld (moving) camera can be uncomfortable for the camera operator. Before you choose this approach, be sure it matches the style and mood of your video.*

What I love about the art of film is that you can use different types of shots within a scene. A play audience can only watch a stage performance from one angle. When they're watching film, your audience can see a wide shot, get closer for a mid shot for the dialogue, and then zoom in for a close-up.

# RECORD SOUND

To record sound when filming, you must use a microphone. A *microphone* recognizes noise and changes the sound into data, which is captured by your camera. You can either use the microphone built into the camera or plug an external microphone into your camera.

*The quality — how good something is — of your video sound can be as important as the picture. Poor sound can be distracting and could make your audience decide not to watch your video.*

*Spend as much time getting your video's sound right as you do getting its picture right. You'll save time when editing later.*

Fixing badly recorded sound in an editing tool is very hard and, in some cases, impossible. If the sound is poor or there's a noise that's impossible to remove, you'll have to rerecord the sound.

## ALL ABOARD WITH THE ONBOARD

An onboard microphone can be useful when you don't have room for an external microphone. A few years ago, I filmed a documentary in Ghana and all I took with me was a camcorder and its onboard microphone. I couldn't use an external microphone because I was the only member of the film crew, and I had to fit all my

filming equipment in my carry-on luggage. It was a challenging experience, but it taught me a lot about recording with onboard microphones.

I've had to do this a few times because of noises that I didn't notice when filming. A big train whistle over dialogue doesn't work, either.

## BUILT-IN MICROPHONE

Because you may have to use a built-in microphone, I explain how to get the best results from one.

*Nearly all digital camcorders and webcams have built-in microphones called* onboard microphones. *They're not the best solution for recording audio or dialogue in videos.*

Recording sound with the onboard microphone on your camera isn't easy, but try using the following techniques to get the best sound.

## GET CLOSE

Sometimes you can't, especially if you're shooting a wide shot, but you may be able to use the sound that you recorded in the close-up shot or mid shot from the same scene.

*You can turn up the level of the onboard microphone, but this increases the overall volume, including background noise.*

## REDUCE CAMERA NOISE

With onboard sound recording, you're more likely to record noise from the camera itself. Such noise may be from the electronics inside the camera, especially when zooming in and out, or it may come from the sounds you make when pressing buttons.

*If you're using the microphone built into your camera, try not to move your hands too much or press buttons when recording. Mounting your camera on a tripod means you don't have to hold or touch the camera as it's recording, which helps reduce noises.*

## REDUCE BACKGROUND NOISE

It isn't easy to control the noises around you, especially if you're filming in a public place, like a park or street. Big-movie film directors can afford to close roads, but you can't. I mean, I assume not.

*Before you start filming, ask the people around you to be quiet for a few minutes so you can hear background noises. Ask people to keep still, too. Even gentle footsteps may be picked up. Other noise could come from cell phones, landline phones, neighbors, pets, clocks, and passing cars.*

You may not have this problem too much if you're filming a vlog or review video in your bedroom, but you may want to warn people in your house that you're filming.

## EXTERNAL MICROPHONE

Recording sound with an external microphone can mean better results than an onboard microphone. You can place your camera in one spot and then scoot closer to your subject or character to record sound. Unwanted background noise gets reduced this way, too.

To use an external microphone when filming, have an extra crew member hold the microphone and pay attention to the sound during filming. This extra crew member is the *sound operator* or *boom operator*.

The external microphone is normally attached to a *boom pole*, which lets the boom operator get the microphone closer to the subject or actor without being in the shot.

*Your boom operator should be able to hold the boom pole for a long time without dropping it. If the boom operator's arm gets tired, the microphone could appear in the shot.*

Ask your boom operator to keep her hands still when holding the boom during filming. The microphone may pick up any tapping or movement on the boom pole.

Some video cameras have a socket on the camera body — either a mini jack or an XLR socket — where you can plug an external microphone.

Jack input          XLR input

When you're recording with an external microphone, try using the following techniques to get the best sound.

## POINT THE MICROPHONE IN THE DIRECTION OF THE SOUND

External microphones are normally *directional* microphones, which means they pick up sound directly in front of the microphone, but not to the sides or behind it. This is good because it will record less background noise.

*With external microphones, it's important to point the microphone where the sound is coming from. If the microphone is pointing away from the action, it won't record the sound you want.*

### POSITION THE EXTERNAL MICROPHONE CORRECTLY

You can position the microphone *above* your subject or *below* it.
The best position depends on what you're filming:

» **Overhead:** Holding the microphone over the scene is the
   most common approach. Overhead microphones are better
   for wider shots and don't pick up noises from your actors'
   hands or feet.

» **Underneath:** Recording sound from underneath is
   mainly used when filming mid shots or close-up shots. Go
   underneath if you have limited room above the actors or to
   shield the microphone from high winds outside.

### AVOID DROPPING THE BOOM IN THE SHOT

A boom pole with an external microphone can feel heavy —
especially if you have to hold it during a long scene. Sometimes
the microphone can drop down into the shot, which means you
have to stop filming.

*Look out for a boom mic creeping into a shot.*

To help avoid the microphone appearing in your shots, ask your boom operator to rest between takes. When you're not filming, the operator can put the boom pole down on the floor — the lower end of the pole.

*Don't put the microphone on the ground! It could damage it.*

# USING A MICROPHONE FOR DIALOGUE

The keys to recording dialogue: Put the microphone as close to your actor as you can (without the microphone being in the shot) and aim the microphone in the direction of the sound.

*The best way to hear unwanted noises is by wearing headphones. Without headphones, you probably won't hear noise until you're importing the footage into the editing tool. If the sound appears in the background in one shot and not in the next, the sound will be uneven between shots. Your audience will notice.*

If you hear a distracting noise — a plane, gust of wind, or passing car — through the headphones when you're filming, stop filming. Wait for the sound to pass, and then retake that shot.

Here are a few ways to avoid unwanted noises during filming:

» **Turn off any air conditioners or fans.** Microphones can pick up noises that sometimes you can't even hear when you're filming.

» **Make sure all cellphones are off.** If you get a call, the shoot has to come to a stop. Sometimes a cellphone's roaming or searching signal can interfere with the camera and wind up on the recorded audio.

» **Don't point the microphone in the direction of any clear background noise.** That includes roads, waterfalls, and fountains. Again, these sounds can come across clearly in the recording and can make it hard to hear dialogue.

» **Don't film in empty rooms.** You'll wind up with lots of echoes in your recording. (But you could *want* echoes in your film.) You can put blankets on walls to help deaden the sound.

## DEAL WITH WIND

Boom operators often have wind problems outside. Not *that* kind of wind — the sky kind of wind!

When you're filming outside, the microphone may pick up noise from the wind, which can make dialogue hard to hear. If you're not sure what this sounds like, try gently blowing on your camera's microphone and listening through the headphones — it isn't a nice sound.

*Wind noise can really only be detected by monitoring the sound using headphones during filming.*

If you can hear wind noise when filming, then you need a windshield. A *windshield* is a furry cover that goes over the microphone to protect it from the wind. You also can get windshields for onboard microphones on video cameras.

Windshields for external microphones come in different types. (You can see why they're sometimes called *dead cats*.)

You can see what external microphones without windshields look like.

If you still have wind noise when filming, try booming from underneath or forming a barrier between the wind and the microphone.

## MONITOR SOUND

*Monitoring* sound is when you listen to the sound being recorded *during* filming. *Checking* sound is when you listen to the sound when watching your footage *after* filming.

*No matter what kind of microphone you're using, it's really important to* monitor *(pay attention to) and check the quality of the sound to see if you picked up any unwanted noises or had issues.*

The best way to do this is with a pair of headphones plugged into your camera or recording device. It's even better to ask someone to listen and monitor the sound during recording. This way you can deal with unwanted noises or trouble right away.

Most camcorders have *audio meters* that let you see how loud or how low the sound is. The audio meters normally are on the LCD monitor on your camcorder. You can use the meter to check sound levels before filming — make sure that the sound you're recording isn't so loud it will distort or isn't so quiet the audience won't be able to hear the dialogue.

Some camcorders let you change microphone levels, but others do it automatically. Either way, make sure you monitor the audio levels before and during filming.

*Before filming, ask your actors to say some of their lines as loudly as they would when you're filming. The bars shouldn't constantly peak (hit the end of the meter, which is usually red). If a meter does this, then the audio levels are too high.*

*Peaking: the danger zone*

If the audio levels are too quiet, on the other hand, then the audio meter bars won't rise as much.

Don't worry if your camera doesn't have any audio meters. In that case, you can always listen to see whether the audio is too loud or too quiet. By plugging headphones into your camera and listening to the dialogue, you'll be able to hear if the audio is too loud, because it will distort and be uncomfortable to listen to. On the other hand, if you can hardly hear what your actor is saying, then you either need to turn up the microphone volume, move the microphone closer to your actor, or ask him or her to speak louder.

## LIGHT YOUR VIDEO

Light is important to your YouTube video. Without light, your audience won't be able to see what you've filmed. Light can also help create a mood or affect your audience's feelings. For example, darker shots can make a scene feel scary or sad.

*Video cameras need more light than our eyes do. Most filmmakers use extra lights to help brighten the actors.*

## USE NATURAL LIGHT

Buying lights for filming can be expensive, but don't worry: You have one of the biggest, most powerful lights available for free — the sun! Sunlight really brightens things up, but as you know, it's only available during the day.

If the sky has just a few (or no) clouds, you'll have direct sunlight. In that case you may see more shadows around and on your subject or actor. You can have the actor look directly into the sun, but bright sunlight can make her squint. Or burn out her retinas completely.

*You can remove some shadows by using a reflector. It helps bounce light back into the darker areas. Photographers use them too. You might have seen a reflector in action when you had school pictures taken.*

You can buy a reflector or you can use anything that has a large white surface, such as a polystyrene board or large posterboard. By angling the reflector toward your subject or actor, the white surface will reflect the sunlight.

*Don't film your actors with the sun behind them.*

She'll be shadowy and you might get *lens flares,* which look like round blobs or streaks of light across your shot. Lens flares can sometimes look great, but they also highlight any dirt or smudges on your camera lens. A cloudy day gives you fewer problems with shadows and lens flares.

You can use daylight to help light scenes in a room (as long as the room has windows). Daylight that's coming through only one window may add shadows to your subject or actor, but you can turn on a lamp or light inside the room.

## USE EXTRA LIGHTS

You have to use extra lights anywhere you're filming without sunlight. If your camera is set to automatic and you're filming a scene with low light, the picture quality will be bad. You may end up with a *grainy* image with lots of dots.

This can look good in some shots, but it's not an effect you want to get accidentally.

*Even if it's an effect you're looking for, it's best to light your video as well as possible and then add effects later, when you're editing.*

You may need extra lights if you're filming a vlog or review using your webcam in your room. Professional lights can be expensive, but you can use lights that you already have around.

*Before you go moving lights around your house, please check with the adult in charge first. You might even ask him or her to help you.*

I didn't have any lights when I first started making films, so I used desk lamps. They were great for close-up shots but usually weren't powerful enough for a wide shot.

» **LED lights:** You can buy inexpensive LED lights, which are brilliant. Smart, sure. But by *brilliant* I mean really bright.

I use camera-mounted LED lights with AA batteries. The LEDs are small and lightweight. I sometimes even take the LED lights outside when I'm filming.

» **Halogen utility lights:** You can buy these from hardware stores for a lot less money than professional lighting.

*Halogen utility lights get hot when you use them. Let them cool down before you move them around. They also use a lot of power, so you may want to ask an adult to help you set them up.*

*The main thing to remember when lighting your YouTube video is to make sure that every shot looks natural. When the scene in your viewfinder doesn't look natural, something is wrong. Look through the viewfinder. You, your subject, or the actors should look much like they look when you look at them directly, without a camera.*

If you're making a vlog, review, or how-to video, shining a desk lamp on your face could provide enough light to make your shot look great. For short films or funny videos that you capture around the house or outside, there may be enough light around so you don't need extra.

Consider this when lighting your video:

» **Overexposed shots:** If shots are *overexposed*, it means they're too bright. Some of the brighter areas may have gone white and lost detail. You can see that parts of his face are completely white and that I've lost some of the detail and color. It's really hard — usually impossible — to put this detail back with editing.

You can overexpose film by placing too much light on your subject or in your scene, or it can happen because the iris on your camera is open too wide or the aperture is set too low.

You can fix this easily by lowering the light or by raising the aperture levels.

» **Underexposed shots:** If your shots are *underexposed*, they're too dark. You may not be able to see some areas of your subject or actor. You can see only part of the face, and I've lost some detail. Underexposure is easier to repair with editing, but it still isn't great having to boost the brightness too much. That can affect the color and wind up grainy.

» **Three-point lighting:** This film and TV lighting technique has three lights set up around the subject or actor. A three-point lighting setup works like this:

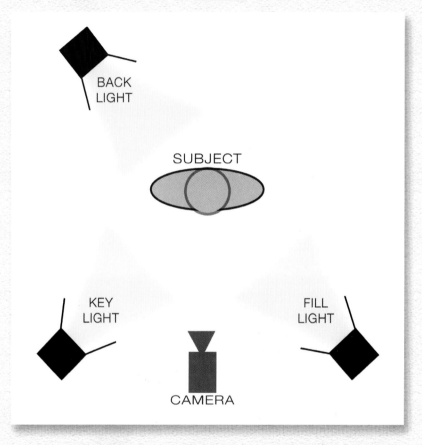

» The *key light* can be on either side of the subject. It gives the most light to the subject. It brightens one side of the subject's face. (The actual light you see on the next page is just a prop.)

» Put the *fill light* on the opposite side to the key light. It fills in light to make fewer shadows on the face. Set the fill light a little lower in brightness than the key light.

» The *back light* is behind the subject to one side. It may seem like it doesn't do anything, but it lights around the head to separate the subject from the background.

And if you want to really go for it, put all three lights together.

» **Bounced light:** This is my favorite technique because it provides the most natural light. *Bounced lighting* reflects light off walls, ceilings, and reflectors and onto a subject. Directly shining a light can cast shadows behind a subject or light up a face too much. Bouncing light off the ceiling, wall, or reflector, however, breaks up the light around the room.

Sometimes I use a mixture of bounced light and direct light to get a reflection in an actor's eyes. It can produce a sharper-looking image.

You can combine a key light with bounced light to reflect light in the actor's eyes.

*If you don't have many lights in the room, you can reflect light onto your subject using tin foil. You could even wrap foil around cardboard to make your own reflector.*

## APER-WHAT?

*Aperture* is the hole in the lens that lets light through. The aperture size is controlled by the *iris,* which is a ring that opens and closes inside the lens (to let in more or less light). The lower the aperture number, the wider the hole, the more light coming through. Most camcorders and webcams have an auto-iris function that measures the amount of light in a scene and changes the aperture setting. Some video cameras let you change aperture manually (to whatever you think it should be), but each camera is different. Read your camera's operating manual.

## DIRECT YOUR FILM

The *director* works with the actors and crew to get the best from them and make sure the story is being told through what they do.

As a director, it's important to have:

» **Good communication skills:** A director usually has in his head an idea what the film should look like. It's your job to get that idea across to the crew and actors. This means you also should be good at communicating and explaining what you want.

» **Confidence:** Directors should be confident about what they want, because the crew and actors need to trust that directors know what they're doing. This includes making decisions. If you want to get an extra shot or re-film something, just do it. I've wasted too many hours wondering if I should film something or not. In the time I wasted, I could've just re-filmed.

» **Attention to detail:** The director needs to be able to focus on the fine detail of the scene. You have to do many things at once: watch the actors, know what the camera operator is doing, and listen to the dialogue.

As a director, it's useful to have the following items with you during filming:

» **Director's monitor:** Often, directors watch a TV monitor that's plugged into the camera so they can see what's happening in the scene.

Don't worry if you don't have one of these monitors. You can direct the scene by looking through the monitor on the camera.

*I think it's easier to watch a scene through a monitor because what the camera sees is normally different from what you see when directly watching a scene. It may sound odd, but your actor's performance can also look very different through a camera.*

» **Script:** Having the script with you is a must. With it, you can check the dialogue and keep track of where you are in the scene. I like to make notes on my script to remind me of things to capture and remind myself of props or costumes I need for a shot.

» **Storyboard or shot list:** With these items you can keep track of shots filmed (and those you need to film). I tend to work mainly from the shot list. I can tick off the shots as they're done, plan the day, and see how well we're sticking to the schedule.

When you're directing, imagine the edit in your head as you go. As you film a shot, place it into an imaginary timeline in your head. Picture how the shots go together. It works! And it helps me think of shots I missed or of extra shots and angles. It also helps to imagine how the story is coming together. Is it working? Do you need to change anything?

*You may be worried. There's so much to think about when directing your YouTube video! Don't fret. You'll learn as you go. These things will become natural to you. Plus, I've been directing for many years and I'm still learning new things.*

## DIRECT YOUR ACTORS

The director works with the actors to help them perform the character in the way the writer imagined. Because the actors can't see themselves — they can't see what they look like while

## BEEN THERE, DONE THAT, GOT THE T-SHIRT

When I first started, I filmed a whole day of footage and didn't check the shots after every scene. When I got around to importing the footage onto my computer, I found that there was an issue with the camera and that the footage was no good. I couldn't use any of the shots that I filmed that day.

I had to arrange the shoot for another day, call the actors and crew back in, and buy them all lunch to say sorry. I'll never do that again. I *always* check the shots after every scene at least.

they're acting — the director offers advice about how to express emotions and say lines.

*Be a nice director. You don't want to be harsh and upset your actors. You'd end up with no one to film.*

## DIRECT YOUR CREW

As a director, it's important to know how the camera works and how to film the types of shots that I explain in Project 2. Knowing this stuff helps you explain to your crew how you want your shots to look.

You'll choose shot types that help express a scene's emotion. For example, which shot would you use if you want to show the fear on someone's face? That's right — you'd use a close-up.

## USE SHOOTING TIPS

It's exciting to get to the point where you can start filming. Using your script and shot list, you can get your equipment and crew and start.

Before you do, these tips will help get the best from your shoot.

### CHECK FOR CONTINUITY MISTAKES

Have you ever watched a film and noticed that the actor picked something up with his left hand, and then in the next shot has it in his right hand? Or noticed a glass of soda that's half full, and then in the next shot is nearly empty? This is a continuity mistake.

 Continuity mistakes *happen when something in a scene, like a prop or actor, changes between shots.*

Blockbusters normally hire someone to look out for continuity mistakes, but even then they happen. Asking your crew and actors to look out for continuity mistakes will reduce how many happen in your film.

Next time you watch a film, look for continuity mistakes. Keep them to yourself, though. You don't want to annoy the people you're watching with. Otherwise, you might end up watching films on your own, like me.

### ALWAYS GET ONE MORE TAKE THAN YOU NEED

You'll probably film the same shot several times. It takes a bit to get the right take, unless you have a perfect cast and crew. (Spoiler: That's not possible.)

A *take* is one recorded performance in a scene. It starts when the camera operator presses the Record button and stops when she stops recording.

*When you get a good take, you can either go to the next shot on your list or get one more take to be safe. Get the extra take. Your actors might perform even better, or there might be a mistake in the last take that you didn't notice.*

If you're recording a vlog, review, or how-to video, you may want to record a few takes and choose the best one.

### SHOOT OUT OF ORDER

Most films are shot out of *sequence,* which means a different order than how they appear in the film. This makes the filming process as simple as possible.

For example, you may want to record all the footage of your cat first and then record your intro. Or maybe film yourself demonstrating a dance before explaining how to do the dance. You're doing the Funky Chicken, right?

## CHECK YOUR SHOTS

The last thing you want is to import your footage at the end of the day and find there are problems and you can't use it. Trust me, I've been there.

*Check your footage after each shot or scene that you film. Make it a habit, even.*

Here's why you should check your footage:

» **Technical issues:** You may have a camera issue or dirt on your lens that you didn't notice during filming. Trust me: You'll notice when you play it back on a larger monitor or import it to your computer.

» **Continuity and mistakes:** You may miss mistakes while filming. Maybe an actor stumbled over a word or something shouldn't be in a shot.

» **Missed shots:** Looking through your footage is a great opportunity to double-check that you filmed everything on your shot list.

*Missing shots is very easy to do and can cause problems during editing. Check your short list.*

Checking your footage is a little more complicated if your camera records with tape instead of media cards.

*After watching the tape footage, make sure you play to the end of the last take. You don't want to record over any of the scenes you already shot. The safest thing to do is record a placeholder at the end of every scene.*

A *placeholder* is just a few seconds of blank video. You might shoot it with the lens cap on. Just be sure you take the cap off for the next shot!

# PROJECT **3** EDIT

***EDITING IS THE ICING ON THE FILM CAKE.*** As you edit, you get to see all your footage together, with effects that make better viewing.

In this project, I show you how to import footage you've captured, cut it together onto a timeline with some cool transitions, and then export it so it's ready to upload to YouTube.

## CHOOSE AN EDITING TOOL

There are tons of editing tools. They offer different effects and work differently, but their basic functions are similar. They allow you to

» Import, or download, footage from your camera or media card.

» Cut and arrange your video footage on a timeline.

» Add transitions.

» Export what's in your timeline to a final movie.

I cover the process in this project.

This project uses iMovie (which is for Apple products) and Movie Maker (which is for Windows operating systems).

» If you have a Macintosh, you can buy iMovie through the App Store for a small amount of money. And it's free for newer Macs (just check in the App Store to see if it shows Free as the price).

» If you have another kind of computer that uses Windows (Dell, HP — basically anything besides a Mac), Movie Maker is your editing tool. If you don't already have Movie Maker on your computer, download it for free from windows.microsoft.com/en-us/windows-live/essentials as part of the Windows Essentials Bundle.

You could buy other editing tools that offer more amazing effects and functions, but the tools I just listed offer more than you need for your first YouTube video, and they cost less.

First I show you how to edit your video in iMovie, and then in Movie Maker. If you have Windows, just skip forward in this project.

## CREATE A NEW EVENT IN IMOVIE

I film a new project nearly every day of the year. If all my footage were in one folder, it would be tough to find previous projects and clips.

*Before you start importing your footage onto your computer, you need to create a new event. An event is how iMovie keeps the footage and the project. It helps you find your clips and timeline the next time you open the program.*

You can create a new event to import your footage into by following these steps:

 **1 Open Applications and click the iMovie icon.**

iMovie opens.

**2 In the iMovie main screen, choose New Event from the File menu.**

**3 Type a name for your video in the Name text box.**

Milo Took My Phone is the name of my video. The Milo Took My Phone event now appears in my iMovie Library list.

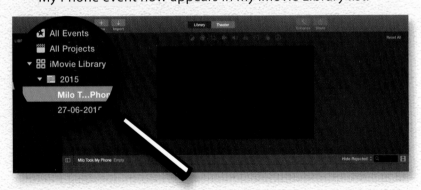

# IMPORT YOUR FOOTAGE IN IMOVIE

After you create your event, you can import your video footage into it. When you import video footage into iMovie, it stores your video clips in a folder on your computer's hard drive.

After you import your clips, you can disconnect your camera or take your media card from your computer.

To import your footage, follow these steps:

**1** **Connect your camera or device to your computer with a USB cable or FireWire cable.**

If you use a media card instead, put it into a media card reader attached to your computer.

The iMovie Import dialog box automatically pops up.

 **2** **If the Import dialog box doesn't automatically appear, click the Import icon in the toolbar.**

Your camera, device, or media card should appear in the Cameras/Devices pane (on the left side of the Import dialog box, shown on the next page).

**3** **Click your card, camera, or device in the Cameras/Devices pane.**

You should see a preview of the first clip. (You can see Milo getting a close-up here.) Under the monitor is a list of the video clips.

**4** Do your thing!

**5** Click the clip(s) you want to import.

**6** Click the Import Selected button in the bottom-right corner of the Import dialog box.

 *When it starts, the import area will close. You should see your clips in the event area.*

# RECORD FROM WEBCAM IN IMOVIE

You can record from your webcam directly into your iMovie event by following these steps:

 **1** In iMovie, click the Import icon.

**2** Click your webcam in the Camera/Devices pane.

You should see a live video preview.

**3** To start recording, click the Record button.

**4** **Do your thing!**

**5** **Click the button below the preview monitor again to stop recording.**

**6** **Click Close in the bottom right.**

The Import dialog box closes. The clip(s) you just recorded should appear with your other video footage in your new event.

## CREATE A NEW TIMELINE IN IMOVIE

After it's imported into your event, you can edit your footage. Before you can edit, however, you must create a timeline.

*A timeline, or project, is where you drag your footage to edit and place your clips into the right order.*

To create your timeline, follow these steps:

**1** **Make sure your event is selected.**

The event name should be highlighted in the Libraries window. If it's not, click your event name in the Libraries window.

**2** **Choose Movie from the New menu.**

You see a dialog box that shows themes.

**3** **Click No Theme. Then click the Create button.**

The Create dialog box appears.

## 4  Name your project and make sure it's being created in your new event.

I named my project Milo
Took My Phone.

Name:  Milo Took My Phone

Event:  Milo Took My Phone

Cancel    OK

As shown on the next
page, your new project
appears above your footage in your event, and the timeline
appears below your footage.

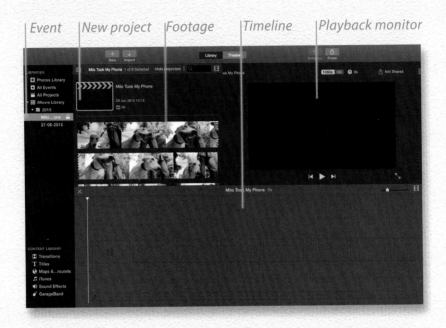

Event | New project | Footage | Timeline | Playback monitor

# ADD FOOTAGE TO A TIMELINE IN IMOVIE

With your timeline created, it's time to add your video footage to it. The great thing about iMovie is that you can easily add clips to your timeline and move them around.

When you're recording your footage, you'll have sections at the beginning and the end of the clips that you don't want to keep. These sections normally include extra material, such as the director shouting orders at actors.

*It might be useful to have your script or shot list in front of you as you edit. This helps you know the order for the clips and makes sure you don't miss any clips.*

You can cut off extra bits when you add your footage to your timeline. Follow these steps:

**1** Make sure your new project timeline is open.

**2** **Hover the cursor over the first video clip you want to use.**

Use the best of the first shot in your shot list.

*When you hover over the footage, you can see a preview in the Playback Monitor dialog box. Hover the cursor over the part of the clip where you would like to start. Then click and drag the cursor to the right. The selection on the clip gets a yellow outline. Don't worry if you let go before you select everything you want to include. Just click either edge and drag to the left or right.*

**3** **Click and hold in the center of the selected clip, drag your selection to the beginning of the timeline, and let go.**

Your selected clip appears in the timeline.

**4** **Hover your cursor over the playback monitor to make sure you have all the footage you want.**

The playback controls appear.

The table tells you what each playback control does.

## PLAYBACK CONTROLS

| Control | What It Does |
|---|---|
| ▶ | This plays the footage in the timeline from where your play head is in the timeline. During playback, this turns into the pause button. |
| ◀ | This button takes you back to the beginning of the clip. If you hold it down, the clip rewinds during playback. |
| ▶ | This button skips to the next clip in the timeline. If you hold it down, the clip fast-forwards during playback. |
| ⤢ | This button plays the footage in the timeline in full screen. Click it again to change it back. |

When you play your clips, a line moves along the timeline. This line is called the *play head.* You can:

» Click the play head and drag it along your timeline.

» Click above a clip to move the play head there.

If you accidentally cut off part of the video at the beginning or end, in the timeline you can make the clip longer.

**5** **Select the clip that you want to extend or shorten, and hover over the beginning or end of the clip.**

The cursor changes to two arrows pointing away from each other. Click and hold, and then move the cursor left or right.

*Sometimes it's hard to get those two arrows to appear in the play head. Be patient.*

**6** **To add your second shot, select the footage you want.**

Use the same steps you used to add your first clip.

**7** **Click and drag the shot to the right of your first clip in the timeline. Then let go.**

This automatically places your second shot after your first.

**8** **Repeat this step again and place the shot to the right side of the second shot.**

**9** **Keep adding clips to your timeline in the order on your shot list.**

*If you need to swap one clip with another, click and drag the clip where you want it. Then let go.*

To remove sound from a video clip, hover over the line between the video and audio within the clip.

Your cursor should turn into two arrows pointing up and down.

**10** **Click and drag the line down to the bottom of the clip.**

The table lists some keyboard shortcuts that can help with editing.

## KEYBOARD SHORTCUTS

| Keyboard Shortcut | What It Does |
| --- | --- |
| Command-I | Imports footage into an event |
| Command-N | Creates new movie project |
| Command-E | Exports a timeline to the iMovie Theatre |
| Spacebar | Plays the video in the timeline from where the play head is |
| Right-arrow key | Moves the play head one frame forward, which helps for precise editing |
| Left-arrow key | Moves the play head one frame backward, which helps for precise editing |
| Down-arrow key | Jumps play head to the beginning of the next clip in the event browser or timeline |
| Up-arrow key | Jumps play head to beginning of current clip or previous clip in the event browser or timeline |
| Forward slash (/) | Plays the selected area of clip in event browser or timeline |
| Backslash (\) | Plays from the beginning of the clip, event, or timeline |
| Shift-Command-F | Plays clip from play head position in full screen |
| Esc | Exits full-screen view |
| Command-Z | Undoes last action or change |
| Shift-Command-Z | Redoes last action or change |
| Command-C | Copies the selected clip or text |
| Command-X | Cuts the selected clip or text |
| Command-V | Pastes the copied clip or text |

# ADD TRANSITIONS IN IMOVIE

With your video footage in the timeline, think about how one video clip joins another. That's a *transition*. A transition can be anything from a simple hard cut to a bit of flashy animation, depending on the type of YouTube video you're creating.

iMovie offers certain kinds of transitions, so add one at the beginning and ending of your video by following these steps:

**1** **Choose Transitions under Content Library at the bottom.**

**2** **Click and drag the transition you want to the beginning of your first clip in the timeline. Then let go.**

A transition icon appears before your first clip.

**3** **Select the first clip and click the Play Clip button in the Playback Monitor dialog box.**

**4** Click and drag the transition to the end of the last clip on the timeline. Then let go.

You can see what this all looks like by moving the play head to the beginning of the timeline and clicking the play button under the playback monitor.

*Use transitions carefully. Using too many can make your video feel long and not professional. Transitions usually show time passing or help change the mood. Using crazy transitions like Mosaic or Spin Out can distract your audience, which isn't a good idea. Keep it simple. Films and TV shows normally use just a few types, like fades and cuts.*

# ADD JUMP CUTS IN IMOVIE

Unwanted footage might show someone thinking of his line or stumbling on a word. Jump cuts are popular and filmmakers often use them even if there isn't much to cut out.

*Jump cuts are common in YouTube videos, especially vlogs or tutorials. Jump cuts are simply hard transitions that shorten a video or cut out any unwanted footage.*

To add jump cuts to your YouTube video timeline, follow these steps.

**1** Make sure your project timeline is open.

**2** Find a section of video in your timeline that you'd like to get rid of.

**3** Click in the timeline where you want to start cutting.

The play head moves to this point in the timeline.

**4** **On the keyboard, press Cmd and then the B.**

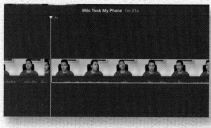

The clip splits.

**5** **Click in the timeline where you want to stop cutting.**

The area is highlighted.

**6** **On the keyboard, press Cmd and then the B.**

**7** **Select the section of footage you want to ditch. On the keyboard, press Delete or Backspace.**

The unwanted footage is removed. Take a look at the video in the timeline to see what your jump cut looks like.

# ADD TITLES IN IMOVIE

*Titles* are words that appear over the footage in a video and give the audience information. Most titles are at the beginning of a video, and they tell the name of the video and information about the filmmakers. (Hey, that's you!)

You can add titles over video or over a blank screen before the clips, or anywhere in your timeline.

For now, start by adding a title at the beginning of your YouTube video:

**1** **Click the Titles button in the Content Library.**

You see a list of titles. To see what the titles look like, click at the beginning of the title thumbnail and press the spacebar.

2 **When you find the title you want to use, click and drag the title onto the start of your timeline.**

I chose the title Expand. When you've dragged the title into the timeline, the preview monitor will show your title with Title Text Here highlighted.

*Choose a title effect that suits your YouTube video style. Also, choose the right amount of time to have it up. Read your title out loud slowly. That's how long it should play.*

If your video is a vlog or tutorial, you may not want a flashy effect. Also think about how long your title plays. Don't make it so short that your audience doesn't have time to read it.

(But don't make it so long that your audience gets bored and falls asleep.)

**3** **Double-click the title in the preview monitor to enter your text.**

**4** **Select the text in your title box and click the Font icon. Select a font from the list.**

A *font* is the way words, numbers, and symbols look.

**5** **To change how big it is, select the text in your title box and click the text size drop-down menu. Select a size.**

**6** **Watch the title in your video by clicking at the start of your timeline and pressing the spacebar.**

# RECORD A VOICEOVER IN IMOVIE

You may want to use a voiceover as part of your YouTube video. As long as you have a microphone or webcam connected to your computer, iMovie's tool for recording voiceovers will work for you.

Before recording your voiceover, keep in mind these simple ways to improve the quality of the audio recording:

» **Make sure it's as quiet as possible.** You may want to let people know that you're recording audio.

» **Check for echoes.** Clap or say a word loudly. Then listen carefully for any echo. If there is one, try another room. A room with carpeting or lots of rugs and sofas is a good bet.

» **Have your mouth about seven inches away from the microphone.** That's about from the end of your thumb to the end of your outstretched little finger. Extend that pinky!

To record the voiceover using iMovie, follow these steps:

**1** **Have your voiceover script ready to read.**

**2** **Move the play head to the point in your timeline where you want to start your voiceover.**

**3** **On your keyboard, press the V key.**

The voiceover recording function opens. If it doesn't open, click Record Voiceover from the Window menu.

 **4** **Click the microphone icon to start recording your voiceover.**

A countdown gives you three seconds before recording. After that, start your voiceover.

Because you're recording, a red and green strip appears underneath your footage.

 **5** **Click the microphone icon to stop recording.**

A voiceover appears below your footage in a green audio box, and the voiceover clip appears as an audio clip in your event. You can trim the beginning and ending of your voiceover.

**6** To trim your voiceover, select it. Then hover your mouse pointer over the beginning or ending of the clip.

**7** When two arrows appear, click and drag left or right to make the clip shorter or longer.

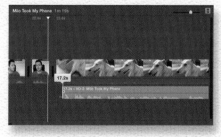

*You can't make a clip longer unless you already trimmed to make it shorter.*

If you want to record another voiceover in your timeline, repeat the steps.

# IMPORT YOUR FOOTAGE INTO A NEW MOVIE MAKER PROJECT

When you first open Movie Maker, a new project is automatically created for you.

*A project is the area of the editing tool where you import and arrange your footage.*

To import video footage into your project, follow these steps:

**1** **Import the footage from your card, camera, or device into a folder on your PC.**

Some cameras come with software (on a DVD) that lets you download the footage from the camera to your computer. The same software will be on the device maker's website.

 **2** **Open Movie Maker from Apps.**

**3** **Click the Click Here to Browse for Videos and Photos link.**

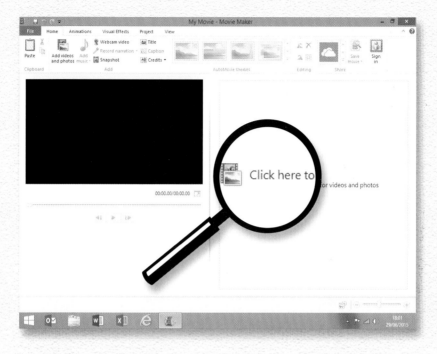

**4** **Go to the folder where your video footage is stored on your computer.**

Each take or clip recorded by your video camera will appear as a separate file. Your camera normally names the files, so they may not make sense.

**5** **Click the file(s) and then click Open.**

The files you select appear in your project timeline as *thumbnails* (small pictures).

*You can choose more than one file by holding down the Ctrl key on your keyboard and clicking the files in the browser.*

**6** **Click File in the toolbar and then click Save Project As.**

**7** **Go to the folder where you want to save your project, type a name, and click Save.**

I like to save my project in the same folder as the video footage.

# I CAN'T SEE MY VIDEO BUT I CAN HEAR IT

Some versions of Movie Maker might give you some trouble. When you try to play your footage, do you hear the sound but see nothing but a black screen? Try these fixes.

Update your computer's video card driver:

**1** In a web browser, visit www.microsoft.com/en-us/windows/compatibility/CompatCenter/Home.

**2** In the search bar, type **Movie Maker device driver**.

**3** Choose the option that fits your situation.

**4** Follow the steps.

Or you can save your video files to your desktop:

**1** In Windows Explorer, find your video files on your computer.

**2** Click and drag your video files to the desktop.

**3** Click the video files and choose Open With.

**4** From the list, choose Movie Maker.

*Save your project often. You never know when Movie Maker might crash, losing all your hard work. If you want to be lazy, you can just press Ctrl+S on your keyboard to save your project.*

**8 To cut out footage from a clip, select the clip and then click the Edit tab.**

This brings up editing options.

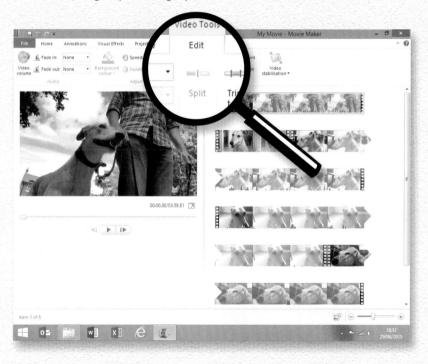

**9 Click Trim Tool.**

Trim sliders show up under the preview monitor. Use them to choose the section you want.

**10** **Move the sliders. When you're happy, click Save Trim.**

» Move the left slider to trim the beginning of the clip.

» Move the right slider to trim the ending of the clip.

This takes you back to the project. You should be able to tell that your clip has been trimmed.

**11** **Repeat the steps for the other clips in your project.**

*You can extend a clip that you've trimmed. Select the clip and click Trim Tool. Adjust the trim sliders and then click Save Trim.*

**12** **To remove sound from a clip, select the clip in the project. Click the Edit tab, and then click Video Volume.**

The volume slider shows up.

**13** **Click and drag the volume slider all the way over to the left.**

**14** **To move footage around, click and drag a clip to the new position.**

# RECORD FROM WEBCAM IN MOVIE MAKER

You can record from your webcam directly into your Movie Maker project timeline. Just follow these steps:

**1** **Click the Home tab in Movie Maker.**

**2** **Click Webcam Video in the ribbon below the toolbar.**

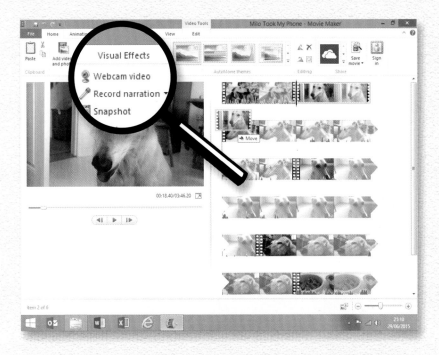

A preview of your webcam should appear. Get ready!

**3** **Click the Record button in the top left when you're ready.**

**4** **Click Stop when you've finished.**

A Save Video dialog box opens.

**5** **Find the folder where you want to save your video. Then type a name in the File Name box.**

**6** **Click Save.**

Your webcam video is added to your project timeline.

# ADD TRANSITIONS IN MOVIE MAKER

When you have your clips where you want them to appear on YouTube, you can add transitions.

A *transition* is how one video clip joins another. A transition can be anything from a simple hard cut to a bit of flashy animation, depending on the type of video you're creating.

You can add Movie Maker transitions to the footage in your project timeline like this:

**1  Click Animations from the top.**

You see different animations and transitions.

*You can hover your cursor over a transition to see how it'll work.*

## 2 Click a clip and then click the transition.

You can test this transition by clicking the first clip and then clicking the play button under the playback monitor.

You can keep adding transitions between other clips. To see what everything looks like, click the first clip and then the play button.

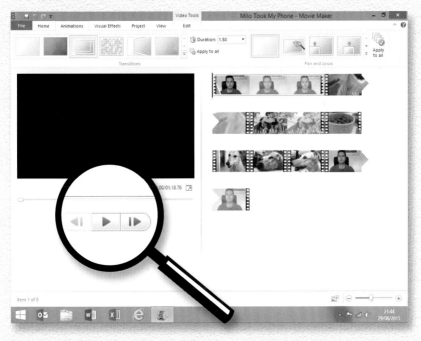

*Use transitions carefully. Using too many can make your video feel long and not professional. Transitions usually show time passing or help change the mood. Using crazy transitions like Mosaic or Spin Out can distract your audience, which isn't a good idea. Keep it simple. Films and TV shows normally use just a few types, like fades and cuts.*

# ADD JUMP CUTS IN MOVIE MAKER

Unwanted footage might be someone thinking of his line or stumbling on a word. Jump cuts are popular and filmmakers often use them even if there isn't much to cut out.

Jump cuts *are simply hard transitions that shorten a video or cut out any unwanted footage. Jump cuts are common in YouTube videos, especially vlogs or tutorials.*

To add jump cuts to your YouTube video timeline, follow these steps:

**1** **Make sure your project timeline is open before you start.**

**2** **Click the Edit button in the toolbar.**

**3** **Find the part that you want to get rid of.**

*To zoom in, click the plus (+) button in the bottom-right corner of the workspace.*

**4** **Drag the play head where you want to start cutting.**

*The* play head *is the line that travels along the project when playing your video.*

**5** **Click the Split button (at the top of the screen).**

The clip splits where you've selected.

**6** **Drag the play head where you want the cut to end. Then click the Split button.**

**7** **Select the footage you want to ditch.**

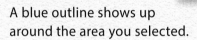

A blue outline shows up around the area you selected.

**8** **Press the Delete key on the keyboard.**

The footage is taken out. Press the play button to see what your jump cut looks like.

# ADD TITLES IN MOVIE MAKER

*Titles* are words that appear over the footage in a video and give the audience information. Most titles are at the beginning of a video, and they tell the name of the video and information about the filmmakers. (Hey, that's you!)

You can add titles over video or over a blank screen before the clips, or anywhere in your timeline.

For now, start by adding a title at the beginning of your video:

**1** **Select the first clip in your project.**

**2** **Click the Home tab in the toolbar, and then click Title below.**

A title is added before the first clip in your project.

**3** **Click the text in the text box. Type your new title.**

*Choose a title effect that suits your YouTube video style. Also, choose the right amount of time to have it up. Read your title out loud slowly. That's how long it should play.*

If your video is a vlog or tutorial, you may not want a flashy effect. Also think about how long your title plays. Don't make it so short that your audience doesn't have time to read it. (But don't make it so long that your audience gets bored and falls asleep.)

**4** **Click the text in the title box. Then click the font menu and choose a font.**

A font is how letters, numbers, and symbols look. **This is one font.** This is a different font.

**5** **To change the size, click the text. Click the drop-down menu and select a size.**

You can type a specific size if you want to.

**6** **Check the title. Click at the start of your project and press the spacebar.**

# RECORD A VOICEOVER IN MOVIE MAKER

You may want to use a voiceover as part of your YouTube video. As long as you have a microphone or webcam connected to your computer, Movie Maker's tool for recording voiceovers will work for you.

Before recording your voiceover, keep in mind these simple ways to improve the quality of the audio recording:

» **Make sure it's as quiet as possible.** You may want to let people know that you're recording audio.

» **Check for echoes.** Clap or say a word loudly. Then listen carefully for any echo. If there is one, try another room. A room with carpeting or lots of rugs or sofas is a good bet.

» **Have your mouth about seven inches away from the microphone.** That's about from the end of your thumb to the end of your outstretched little finger. Extend that pinky!

To record the voiceover using Movie Maker, follow these steps:

**1** Have your voiceover script ready to read.

**2** Move the play head where you want to start your voiceover.

**3** Click the Home button in the toolbar. Then click Record Narration.

**4** Click the Record button and start your voiceover.

The video will play.

**5** Click the Stop button to quit recording.

The Save Narration dialog box opens.

**6** Find the folder where you want to save your voiceover.

**7** **Type a name in the File Name box and click Save.**

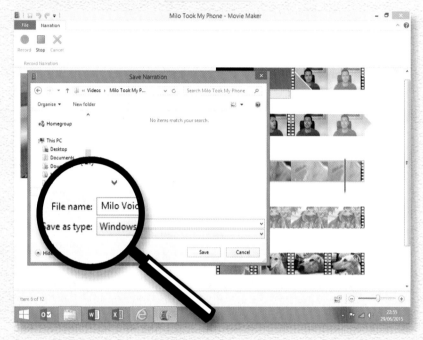

Your voiceover shows up underneath the video in the project. To record another voiceover in your timeline, repeat the steps.

# PROJECT 4 SHARE

***SHOWING YOUR VIDEO TO YOUR FAMILY AND FRIENDS IS GREAT.***
But you may want to share it with even more people. YouTube is
the perfect place to do that. The website gets billions of views
every day, and some of its videos have been viewed hundreds of
millions of times.

In this project I show you how to set up a YouTube channel and
upload your video to YouTube. The steps that you take depend
on whether you edited your video in iMovie, Movie Maker, or in
another program.

## SET UP A YOUTUBE CHANNEL

Before you can upload your video to YouTube, you need to create
a Google account and a YouTube channel. Uploading your video
to YouTube is like saving your video to the website so other
people can watch it whenever they want.

*In most countries you have to be aged 13 or older to set up a Google account. Get permission from a parent or guardian before you start. They might even be able and willing to help.*

These steps assume that you don't already have a Google account. If you already have one, go to www.youtube.com and skip to Step 5. Follow these steps to set up your YouTube channel:

**1** **Go to www.youtube.com.**

**2** **Click Sign In.**

Sign In is in the top-right corner of the YouTube home page.

**3** **Click the Create Account button.**

It's below the Sign In form.

**4** **Fill in the Create Your Google Account form. Then click Next Step.**

You're asked to verify your new account (let Google know it's actually your email address). A verification email goes to the email address you entered in the form.

**5** **Open the email from Google. Then click the link in it.**

The link opens the Google account login page.

**6** **Sign in by filling in your email address and password.**

 *If you're younger than 13 years old, stop right there! Ask your parents to set up an account.*

**7** **Go back to the YouTube home page.**

YouTube automatically sets up a channel with your name.

## 8 Click your profile icon.

Your icon is in the top-right corner of the YouTube home page.

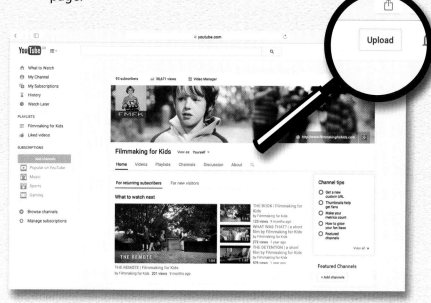

## 9 Click the YouTube Settings icon. Under Additional Features, click Create a New Channel.

You may be asked to verify your identity. If so, follow the steps to verify your account.

After verifying your account, you may need to go back to Step 8.

## 10 Type a name for your new channel.

*Don't use your real name as a channel name.*

Choose a channel name that's related to your style of videos. Sometimes the most random and crazy channel names are the most popular.

**11** **Click the up or down arrow and choose a category.**

The category you choose depends on what kinds of videos you make.

» Product or Band is for music videos and branded product videos.

» Company, Institution, or Organization is for business, education, and charity videos.

» Arts, Entertainment, or Sports is for short films, sports, funny videos, TV, dance, and gaming videos.

» Other is for any video that isn't in the other categories. This could include vlogs and tutorials.

**12** **Click in the box beside I Agree to the Pages Terms.**

*This is like signing a contract between Google and you. You may want your parents to read this before you click the box.*

**13** **Click Done.**

You're ready to start uploading videos to your new channel.

## UPLOAD A VIDEO TO YOUTUBE

These steps are for you if you *didn't* use iMovie or Movie Maker to edit your video:

**1** **Go to www.youtube.com and log in to your YouTube account.**

**2** **Click Upload.**

### 3 Click Select Files to Upload and find your video file.

### 4 Click Choose.

Your video starts uploading. A progress bar shows the upload process.

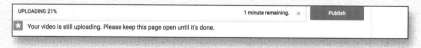

### 5 Enter your video's title and description.

*Choosing a good title can get more views for your video. What would make you want to watch your video? Is it* The Funniest Video Ever? *Does it help people* Dance Like Michael Jackson? *Your title should have to do with what's in your video, but it also should stand out.*

**6 Add tag words if you want to.**

Read more about tag words in the "Tag — You're It!" sidebar later in this project.

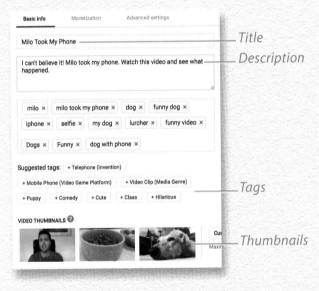

Title

Description

Tags

Thumbnails

**7 Choose a thumbnail from the three below the tags box.**

*Thumbnails* are small still images that appear in the search results for your audience. The thumbnail is like a preview of what's in your video.

*Choose a thumbnail that represents your film the best.*

**8  Click Publish in the top-right corner of the page.**

Your video is on YouTube! When it's published, YouTube will send you an email with the link to your video.

**9  Share this link with your family and friends.**

*You can change your channel's category, decide who can comment on your video, and change other settings. For those steps, see the "Change Your Video Settings" section later in this chapter.*

# SHARE YOUR VIDEO TO YOUTUBE WITH IMOVIE

Follow these steps if you edited your video in iMovie and want to upload the video to YouTube:

**1  Make sure you have a YouTube account.**

*Hey you! Yes, you. You have to be at least 13 years old to have a YouTube account. Ask your parents for permission to use one of their accounts, or ask for help setting up one. Setting up an account, that is — not setting up your parents.*

**2  Open your video in iMovie.**

**3  Click Share in the top toolbar.**

You get a list of sharing options.

## TAG — YOU'RE IT!

*Tag words* are related to your video. They
help people search for it. When you're
thinking about what tags to use, think
about how people might find your video. How would
you look for your own video? What words would you
enter? What words are related to it? Is it a *funny video*,
a *documentary*, or a *short film*? Is there a *cat jumping*
or *dog snoring* in it? Or a *place* or *landmark*? Don't use
unrelated words. That could confuse people and make
you lose viewers.

**4**  **Click the YouTube logo.**

You see the settings for your video.

**5**  **Click in the title box and type a new title if you want to.**

**6**  **Add a description about the film by clicking in the
description box.**

**7**  **Add tag words if you want to.**

If you do, put a comma in between the words or phrases. If
you want help thinking up tag words, read the "Tag — You're
It!" sidebar in this project.

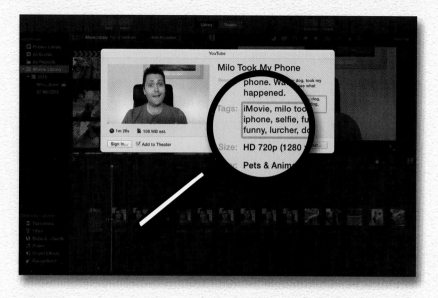

 *You can choose the size of your video. It's best to leave it at the default (automatic) setting.*

**8** **Choose something from the Category menu.**

**9** **From the Privacy menu, choose Public.**

 *You can leave Privacy set to Private if you only want people you know to see your film. But keep in mind that anything you put online isn't very private. If you want your video to be found by anyone, then change your privacy settings to Public. Check with your parents first before setting your video to Public.*

**10** **Leave the Add to Theatre box just like it is.**

**11** **Click the Sign In button.**

**12** **Sign into your account. Then click Sign In.**

**13** Click Next.

**14** Read the YouTube Terms of Service. If you agree, click the Publish button.

Your video is uploaded to your account on YouTube. When it's done, you get a message in the top-right corner of the screen.

To change your title, tags, who can comment on your video, and other settings, jump to the "Change Your Video Settings" section later in this project.

## SHARE YOUR VIDEO TO YOUTUBE WITH MOVIE MAKER

Follow these steps if you edited your video in Movie Maker and want to upload the video to YouTube:

**1** Make sure you have a YouTube account.

*You probably know the score by now: If you're younger than 13 years old, ask your parents for permission to use their accounts. You might have to ask your parents to set up an account.*

**2** Open your video in Movie Maker.

**3** Click the Home tab in the toolbar.

**4** Find Share and click the YouTube logo.

You see video size options.

**5** Select 1920 x 1080.

**6** Sign into your account using the form. Then click Sign In.

You can see the options for your video.

**7** Click in the Title box and type a new title if you want to.

**8** Click in the Description box and describe your video.

**9** Add tag words if you want to.

If you do, put a comma in between the words or phrases. If you want help thinking up tag words, read the "Tag — You're It!" sidebar in this project.

**10** Choose from the Category menu.

**11** Leave the Permission setting as Public.

*You can leave Permission at Private if you want to keep people you don't know from watching your film. But keep in mind that anything you put online isn't very private. If you want your video to be found by everyone, then change your privacy settings to Public. Please check with your parents before setting your video to Public.*

**12 Read the YouTube Terms of Service. If you agree to these terms, click the Publish button.**

Your video uploads to your account on YouTube. A dialog box shows how your upload is going.

## CHANGE YOUR VIDEO SETTINGS

After your video is uploaded to YouTube, you can change the title, description, tags, category, and privacy.

To get to these settings, follow these steps:

**1 Log in to your YouTube account.**

**2 Click your profile icon.**

It's in the top-right corner of the YouTube page.

**3 Click Creator Studio.**

**4 Click Video Manager in the left pane.**

Your videos should be listed.

**5** **Click Edit next to the video whose settings you want to change.**

A new page shows your video with two setting options underneath. The Basic Info tab should be selected. Here's where you can change your title, description, tags, and privacy.

**6** **After you make your changes, click Save Changes.**

It's in the top-right corner of the page.

**7** **Click the Advanced Settings tab underneath your video.**

You see options to change comment settings and the category of your video.

**8** **Click the drop-down list next to Allow Comments and choose Approved.**

*I recommend changing the Allow Comments settings so you can check and approve all the comments that people make about your video before they show up under your video on YouTube.*

**9** **Click the drop-down list next to Category. Select a new category.**

**10** **Click one of the thumbnails next to your video.**

**11** **Click Save Changes.**

*If you don't click Save Changes, the choices you made won't work.*

Your YouTube video is ready to share.

# GET MORE VIEWS

*Have you ever wondered how some videos get so many views? You have lots of tricks for increasing your video's number of* views — *how many people watch it.*

Here are a few tricks to get more views:

» **A title that catches your eye:** The title is one of the first things people see when they're *browsing* (looking for) videos to watch. A catchy title could stop someone in her tracks. What would make someone want to watch your video? Before you decide, look at the titles of the most popular videos on YouTube.

» **A great description:** Lots of people don't include a description, but a good one can make a difference. Your description should explain what the audience will see when watching your video. Keep it to a few sentences. Here's a chance to sell your video.

» **The best tags:** *Tags* are words that people use for searching. Using smart tags increases the chance of people finding your video. Use words from your title and description, plus any words that are related to what happens in your video.

» **Tell everyone:** Be proud of your video! Tell people about it. Email and share your YouTube video link with your friends and family and ask them to share it too.

» **Get subscribers:** Ask people to subscribe to your YouTube channel. Consider subscribing to other YouTube users. Sometimes if you subscribe to other people's channels, they return the favor. If not, ask them. More subscribers means more views.

» **Ask people to like and share:** You can post comments on videos that are similar to yours. Ask people to watch your video and to like and share. This is also a great way to get people to subscribe to your channel.

*Don't go* spamming *(making way too many comments on other people's videos). You could make enemies pretty quickly.*

» **Make playlists:** A *playlist* is a bunch of videos that play, one after the other. A playlist could have videos that are related by subject (like, oh I don't know, dogs) from you and other YouTubers. If your video is about your dog, think about making a playlist with all the funniest dog videos you can find and then include yours.

» **Create annotations:** You may have seen words pop up when you're watching a YouTube video. These are *annotations*. They're normally at the end of a YouTube video and usually say things like "Check out my latest video" or "Subscribe" or "Thumbs up." By adding annotations, you can link to other videos, playlists, and your channel.

» **A good channel image:** Add an image to your channel that grabs the people who are browsing YouTube. Choose an image that goes with the videos in your channel. It could be a screenshot from one of your films or a picture of the cat that stars in your video.

# GLOSSARY

*AS YOU READ THROUGH THIS BOOK, SOME WORDS WILL BE NEW TO YOU.* If you're not sure about a word I've used in this book, you can refer to this list.

**action**   A term called by the director during the filming of a scene to let cast and crew know that a take has started.

**angle**   The position of the camera with respect to the subject.

**audio**   The sound that is recorded when filming.

**blockbuster**   A *large-scale* (really, really big) film with a high production *budget* (lots of money to spend making it) and usually released globally into theaters.

**boom**   A long pole with a microphone attached. Booms are usually held above the actors to record sound in a scene.

**camcorder**   A video camera, which is a device used to record footage.

**camera phone**   A cellphone device that can capture still images and record video footage.

**cast**   The group of actors who are in a film or video.

**character**   A person in a story, usually fictional.

**clapperboard**   A board where you write the details of the film shoot. You hold it in front of the camera to introduce a scene during filming. Traditionally chalk was used to write the details, but now marker pens are used. A clapperboard is sometimes referred to as a *slate*.

**crew**   A group of people behind the scenes or behind the camera who are involved in the making of a film or video.

**cut**   A term called by the director during filming to let the cast and crew know that a take is over.

**development**   The process of building and creating a film.

**dialogue**   The words spoken by the characters in a film or video.

**director**   The person who tells the actors and crew what to do. The director also chooses camera angles and what shots to use in the video.

**editing**   The process of putting the film footage and clips together after filming.

**editing tool**   The software on a computer used to edit video.

**effect**   A visual or audio technique used to enhance or change the look or sound of a video clip. You can add effects during filming or editing.

**establishing shot**   This is the first shot to appear in a new scene, so it sets up, or *establishes*, the scene.

**filmmaker**   The person who creates a film or movie.

**fictional**   Based on a story that is imagined by the writer and not normally based on fact.

**FireWire cable**   A way of transferring data and video footage from a camera to a computer. FireWire connections can also be referred to as *IEEE 1394*.

**focus**   The sharpness of an image.

**frame**   A single image taken from the many images captured within footage. Also known as a *still*.

**import**   Saving video footage to a computer from a camera, tape, or media card.

**lens**   A device attached to the camera that uses glass to focus on a subject.

**lighting**  To provide light to a scene. Also, lighting includes the devices (like a lamp) that provide light to a scene.

**lines**  *Dialogue* (words) in the script performed by the actors.

**location**  A place or area used to film a scene.

**media card**  A small storage device that stores the audio or video being recorded by the camera. CompactFlash (CF), Secure Digital (SD), MicroSD, MiniSD, and SxS cards are some of the media cards for video cameras.

**microphone**  A device used to record sound when filming. Also called a *mic*.

**monitor**  A mini screen that lets you see what the camera captures as it films and review what you have recorded.

**nonfictional**  A film or video using facts or real events starring the actual people involved in the events.

**post-production**  The work you put into a movie after filming.

**prop**  Any item used by an actor.

**reel**  A length of filmstrip wrapped around a metal wheel for viewing on a projector. Film was used to record movies before the age of digital video (and is still used sometimes). Even digital movies are often sent to theaters on film reels. An average movie requires three to five reels of film.

**scene**  A series of shots filmed at one location to tell a section of the story.

**schedule**  A plan of the day's filming that shows the times and details of shots to be filmed.

**script**  A document with details of a story to film, including the scenes and dialogue.

**set**  An area built where a scene can be filmed.

**shoot**  To *film*, or record, video footage.

**shot**   One section of footage recorded by the camera from start to finish.

**shot list**   A list used by the crew showing the shots to be filmed within a scene.

**sound effects**   Sounds added to a film when editing.

**storyboard**   A *series,* or a bunch, of images created before filming. It helps you plan the shots to film.

**subject**   The person or object being filmed.

**take**   One recorded performance of a scene during filming. Expect to shoot tens or hundreds of takes per scene (depending on how long the scene is).

**upload**   Sending and saving a video from a computer to a website or server.

**USB cable**   A cord you can attach to transfer footage from a camera to a computer.

**voiceover**   A recorded voice used in a film or documentary. The speaker is not shown.

**zoom**   Magnifying an object or subject when filming. Makes the subject appear closer or farther away.

# ABOUT THE AUTHOR

Nick Willoughby is a UK-based filmmaker, director, actor, and writer who has a real enthusiasm and love for film. Nick's passion for filmmaking started when he wrote his first short film at the age of 18. Since then, he's been inspiring young people to bring their stories to life through the art of film.

Nick started his career as an actor and went on to experience a wide range of roles within the media industry, from camera operator to director. After offering his skills to schools as a film tutor and consultant, he set up Filmmaking for Kids, which aims to encourage and inspire young people to develop their creativity through the art of film. Nick now facilitates the courses at Filmmaking for Kids while writing and directing films, corporate videos, and commercials with his UK production company, 7 Stream Media.

# AUTHOR'S ACKNOWLEDGMENTS

To be asked to write another book, *Making YouTube Videos*, was an honor and a surprise. It's only fair I acknowledge those who helped me along the way.

You wouldn't have this book in your hand if it wasn't for the inspiration of executive editor Steve Hayes and the support from the fantastic Tonya Cupp.

A big thank you to the handsome Toby for appearing in project opener images. Thank you also to Poppy for being the camera operator, and to Ashish, Josh, and Paige, who appear in some of the figures throughout the book.

I also want to thank my dog Milo for agreeing to star in the YouTube video that accompanies this book. He is just the cutest dog ever and gives the best hugs — not so keen on the sloppy kisses though.

I am especially grateful to my parents for making me who I am. Without their love, support, patience, and constructive criticism I would not be where I am today.

Lastly, I want to thank God for giving me my creative brain and for being my strength and inspiration.

# PUBLISHER'S ACKNOWLEDGMENTS

**Executive Editor:** Steven Hayes

**Development Editor:**
Tonya Maddox Cupp

**Special Help:** Christine Corry,
Fritz Wilbur Henderson

**Sr. Editorial Assistant:** Cherie Case

**Project Layout:** Galen Gruman

**Creative Director:** Paul Dinovo

**Marketing:** Melisa Duffy,
Lauren Noens, Raichelle Weller

**Launch Consultants:** John Helmus,
John Scott